Logan

by Iain Gray

PUBLISHING

WRITING *to* REMEMBER

79 Main Street, Newtongrange,
Midlothian EH22 4NA
Tel: 0131 344 0414
E-mail: info@lang-syne.co.uk
www.langsyneshop.co.uk

Design by Dorothy Meikle
Printed by Printwell Ltd
© Lang Syne Publishers Ltd 2023

All rights reserved. No part of this publication may be reproduced, stored or introduced into a retrieval system, or transmitted in any form or by any means (electronic, mechanical, photocopying, recording or otherwise) without the prior written permission of Lang Syne Publishers Ltd.

ISBN 978-1-85217-764-5

Logan

MOTTO:
This is the valour of my ancestors

CREST:
A heart pierced with a passion nail

TERRITORIES:
Ayrshire, East Lothian, Berwickshire

NAME variations include:
Loganaich *(Gaelic)*
Loggan

Chapter one:

The origins of the clan system

by Rennie McOwan

The original Scottish clans of the Highlands and the great families of the Lowlands and Borders were gatherings of families, relatives, allies and neighbours for mutual protection against rivals or invaders.

Scotland experienced invasion from the Vikings, the Romans and English armies from the south. The Norman invasion of what is now England also had an influence on land-holding in Scotland. Some of these invaders stayed on and in time became 'Scottish'.

The word clan derives from the Gaelic language term 'clann', meaning children, and it was first used many centuries ago as communities were formed around tribal lands in glens and mountain fastnesses.

The format of clans changed over the centuries, but at its best the chief and his family held the land on behalf of all, like trustees, and the ordinary clansmen and women believed they had a blood relationship with the founder of their clan.

There were two way duties and obligations. An inadequate chief could be deposed and replaced by someone of greater ability.

Clan people had an immense pride in race. Their relationship with the chief was like adult children to a father and they had a real dignity.

The concept of clanship is very old and a more feudal notion of authority gradually crept in.

Pictland, for instance, was divided into seven principalities ruled by feudal leaders who were the strongest and most charismatic leaders of their particular groups.

By the sixth century the 'British' kingdoms of Strathclyde, Lothian and Celtic Dalriada (Argyll) had emerged and Scotland, as one nation, began to take shape in the time of King Kenneth MacAlpin.

Some chiefs claimed descent from ancient kings which may not have been accurate in every case.

By the twelfth and thirteenth centuries the clans and families were more strongly brought under the central control of Scottish monarchs.

Lands were awarded and administered more and more under royal favour, yet the power of the area clan chiefs was still very great.

The long wars to ensure Scotland's

independence against the expansionist ideas of English monarchs extended the influence of some clans and reduced the lands of others.

Those who supported Scotland's greatest king, Robert the Bruce, were awarded the territories of the families who had opposed his claim to the Scottish throne.

In the Scottish Borders country – the notorious Debatable Lands – the great families built up a ferocious reputation for providing warlike men accustomed to raiding into England and occasionally fighting one another.

Chiefs had the power to dispense justice and to confiscate lands and clan warfare produced a society where martial virtues – courage, hardiness, tenacity – were greatly admired.

Gradually the relationship between the clans and the Crown became strained as Scottish monarchs became more orientated to life in the Lowlands and, on occasion, towards England.

The Highland clans spoke a different language, Gaelic, whereas the language of Lowland Scotland and the court was Scots and in more modern times, English.

Highlanders dressed differently, had different

customs, and their wild mountain land sometimes seemed almost foreign to people living in the Lowlands.

It must be emphasised that Gaelic culture was very rich and story-telling, poetry, piping, the clarsach (harp) and other music all flourished and were greatly respected.

Highland culture was different from other parts of Scotland but it was not inferior or less sophisticated.

Central Government, whether in London or Edinburgh, sometimes saw the Gaelic clans as a challenge to their authority and some sent expeditions into the Highlands and west to crush the power of the Lords of the Isles.

Nevertheless, when the eighteenth century Jacobite Risings came along the cause of the Stuarts was mainly supported by Highland clans.

The word Jacobite comes from the Latin for James – Jacobus. The Jacobites wanted to restore the exiled Stuarts to the throne of Britain.

The monarchies of Scotland and England became one in 1603 when King James VI of Scotland (1st of England) gained the English throne after Queen Elizabeth died.

The Union of Parliaments of Scotland and England, the Treaty of Union, took place in 1707.

Some Highland clans, of course, and Lowland families opposed the Jacobites and supported the incoming Hanoverians.

After the Jacobite cause finally went down at Culloden in 1746 a kind of ethnic cleansing took place. The power of the chiefs was curtailed. Tartan and the pipes were banned in law.

Many emigrated, some because they wanted to, some because they were evicted by force. In addition, many Highlanders left for the cities of the south to seek work.

Many of the clan lands became home to sheep and deer shooting estates.

But the warlike traditions of the clans and the great Lowland and Border families lived on, with their descendants fighting bravely for freedom in two world wars.

Remember the men from whence you came, says the Gaelic proverb, and to that could be added the role of many heroic women.

The spirit of the clan, of having roots, whether Highland or Lowland, means much to thousands of people.

Meanwhile, many families proudly boast the heraldic device known as a Coat of Arms,.

The central motif of the Coat of Arms would originally have been what was sometimes borne on the shield of a warrior to distinguish himself from others on the battlefield.

Clan warfare produced a society where courage and tenacity were greatly admired

Chapter two:

Ancestral valour

A clan that features prominently in Scotland's frequently turbulent historical record, the Logan name is territorial in designation – derived as it is from the lands of Logan near Auchinleck, East Ayrshire.

But they were not confined to this one particular area, appearing on record elsewhere throughout the Lowlands and they are also thought to have had a link with the Highland Clan MacLennan.

This MacLennan link, however – based on a number of factors including that the Logans and the MacLennans share the same tartan – should not overshadow the fact that both clans have their own distinctly proud heritage, history and traditions.

Early records of the name, including in the now redundant form 'Logyn', appear in the form of signatories at Berwick in 1296 to a humiliating treaty of fealty to England's conquering King Edward I, known as the Hammer of the Scots.

Signed by 1,500 Scottish earls, bishops and burgesses, the parchment is known as the *Ragman*

Roll because of the profusion of ribbons that dangle from the seals of the signatories.

These include Thurbrandus de Logyn, from Dumfriesshire, Phelippe de Logyn, a burgess from Montrose, Wautier Logan, from Lanarkshire and Andreu de Logan from Wigtonshire.

Scotland had been thrown into crisis ten years earlier with the death of Alexander II and the death four years later of his successor, the Maid of Norway, who died while en route to Scotland to take up the crown.

John Balliol was controversially enthroned at Scone as King of Scots in 1292 – fatefully for the nation it had asked the powerful Edward I to arbitrate in the bitter dispute over the succession to the throne, and the hapless Balliol had found himself Edward's chosen man.

The Scots rose in revolt against the imperialist designs of Edward in July of 1296 but the ruthless monarch brought the entire nation under his subjugation little less than a month later, garrisoning strategic locations throughout the length and breadth of the nation, and demanding the signing of the *Ragman Roll*.

Subjugation under the iron fist of English

occupation did not sit well with the proud Scots, however, and the great patriot William Wallace raised the banner of revolt in May of 1297.

A charismatic leader and an expert in the tactics of guerrilla warfare, Wallace and his hardened band of freedom fighters set Scotland aflame – boosting the morale of their fellow countrymen as they inflicted a stunning series of defeats on the English garrisons.

This culminated in the liberation of practically all of Scotland following the battle of Stirling Bridge, on September 11, 1297.

But, defeated at the battle of Falkirk on July 22, 1298, after earlier being appointed Guardian of Scotland, Sir William Wallace was eventually betrayed and captured seven years later, and brutally executed in London as a 'traitor' on August 23, 1305.

His execution only served to further inflame Scottish patriotism, however, and the cause of the nation's freedom was taken up again, this time under the inspired leadership of the great warrior king Robert the Bruce, who had been enthroned as king at Scone in March of 1306.

Over the next eight long years, Bruce and his band of loyal supporters such as the Logans paid dearly for their support of the king – with a Dominus Walter Logan taken prisoner and hanged in the presence of Edward I at Durham in 1306.

But tragedies such as this were outweighed by an astonishing series of successes that had the occupying English forces reeling.

By the summer of 1314, the strategically important and mighty bastion of Stirling Castle was still in English hands, under the command of Sir Philip de Mowbray.

Bruce's younger brother Edward, had agreed to a pledge by Mowbray that if the castle was not relieved through battle by midsummer of the following year, then he would surrender.

This made battle inevitable, and by June 23 of 1314 the two armies faced one another at Bannockburn, in sight of the castle.

It was on this day that Bruce killed the English knight Sir Henry de Bohun in single combat, but the battle proper was not fought until the following day, shortly after the rise of the midsummer sun.

The English cavalry launched a desperate but futile charge on the densely packed ranks of Scottish spearmen known as schiltrons, and by the time the sun had sank slowly in the west the English army had been totally routed, with King Edward II only narrowly managing to make his escape from the carnage of the battlefield.

Bruce died on June 7, 1329 at his manor house of Cardross, near Dumbarton and, before being embalmed and interred with great pomp and ceremony at Dunfermline Abbey, his sternum was sawn open and his heart extracted.

It had long been his wish to undertake a crusade to the Holy Land and, having failed in this, his final instruction was that his heart be carried instead to be placed before the Holy Sepulchre in Jerusalem, and then returned to Scotland to be buried in Melrose Abbey, in the Borders.

Accordingly, his loyal follower Sir James Douglas put the embalmed heart in a casket, placing it on a chain around his neck and entrusting the key to Sir Symon Locard (Lockhart) of Lee.

They then left Scottish shores along with others faithful to Bruce's wishes who included the brothers Sir Robert Logan and Sir Walter Logan, Sir William Keith and Sir William Sinclair of Roslin.

But a European crusade to the Holy Land never materialised. Instead Sir James and his band sailed for Spain where King Alfonso XI of Castile was set to mount a campaign against the Moorish kingdom of Granada.

The battle-hardened Scots were gratefully welcomed and, in August of 1330 formed part of Alfonso's Christian army that was besieging the castle of Teba.

In a vicious battle against the foe, Sir James Douglas and his compatriots were surrounded and most of them killed – including Douglas and the Logan brothers – but not before Douglas had hurled the precious casket before him, shouting: "Lead on brave heart, I'll follow thee" or, as other accounts state: "Go first as thou hast always done."

The casket and Sir Douglas's body were recovered from the carnage of the battlefield by Sir Symon Locard and the few Scots who had survived and returned to Scotland – where, in accordance with Bruce's wishes, his embalmed heart was buried in Melrose Abbey, with Douglas's bones also interred there.

But Bruce's heart was not destined to rest in peace.

Archaeologists excavating the grounds of the by-then ruined abbey in 1921 discovered a casket buried there, and then reburied it in an unmarked spot.

In 1996, an archaeological team from Historic Scotland (now Historic Environment Scotland) excavated a lead container while working on the floor of the abbey's chapter house.

A small hole was carefully drilled in the container and a fibre-optic probe inserted to examine what was inside. The casket was then opened to reveal another, smaller, lead container, with an inscribed copper plaque stating:

"The enclosed leaden casket containing a heart was found beneath Chapter House floor, March 1921, by His Majesty's Office of Works."

The casket was found to contain human tissue and Richard Welander, one of the experts who examined it, stated that although it was not possible to prove with certainty that the casket contained the remains of Bruce's heart, it was reasonable to assume so.

The casket was reburied in a private ceremony at the abbey on June 22, 1998 and, in a more public ceremony held on June 24, the anniversary of the battle of Bannockburn, when Donald Dewar, Secretary of State for Scotland, unveiled a sandstone marker with the inscription by the fourteenth century poet John Barbour, author of the epic The Bruce:

A Noble Hart May Have Nane Ease Gif Freedom Failye (A noble heart can know no ease without freedom)

Mr Dewar, who described the ceremony as one of great significance and symbolism for the people of Scotland, added: "There is a strong and proper presumption that this is the heart, but in a sense it does not matter.

"The casket and the heart are symbols of the man".

Fittingly, meanwhile, the Coat of Arms of Clan Logan features the crest of a heart pierced with a passion nail and the motto *This is valour of my ancestors*.

Chapter three:

Mystery and conspiracy

The east coast of Scotland, rather than Ayrshire, became the main territory of the Logans in 1382 when Sir John de Lestalric died and left his estate to his daughter Katharine and her husband Sir Robert Logan.

Now a small suburb on the outskirts of Edinburgh, west of Craigentinny, 'Lestalric', the estate, became better known as 'Restalrig', meaning 'ridge of the miry land' and it was here that the Logans established themselves in a castle, or tower house, that is now the site of Lochend House, overlooking Lochend Loch.

Destroyed by fire in the late sixteenth century, parts of the tower house form part of Lochend House, a Category B listed building in the care of Edinburgh City Council.

By about 1598 the forbidding stronghold of Fast Castle had come into the possession of Sir Robert Logan's descendant, known as Sir Robert Logan of Restalrig, notorious for his dissolute lifestyle, and who in a later century the antiquarian Sir Walter Scott described as "godless, drunken and deboshed" and "one of the darkest characters of that dark age."

Born in about 1555, the coastal fortress of Fast Castle that he inherited – now in ruins – perched above the North Sea coast in Berwickshire, about four miles (6.4km) northwest of the present-day village of Coldingham.

Built on the site of what had been a fortified position since at least the Iron Age and standing on a narrow, sloping plateau with cliffs up to 148ft (45 metres) rising up on either side from the sea, it was well-nigh impregnable.

Access could only be gained across a drawbridge over a narrow ravine, while a pulley system with a basket provided the only means of access from the sea – although ingress may also have been possible by means of caves at the bottom of the cliffs.

Originally known as 'Fause' (False) Castle because lights would be displayed from it to lure unsuspecting mariners towards the rocks where teams of wrecking parties lay in wait to loot the vessels, it is thought to have been the inspiration for Sir Walter Scott's 'Wolf's Crag' in his novel *The Bride of Lammermoor*.

Also once the property of the Home family the

site, lying just outside St Abb's Head National Nature reserve, is now maintained and protected as a Scheduled Monument by the National Trust for Scotland. Many curious legends attach themselves to the site, which still exudes an air of menacing mystery to this day.

In 1594, Sir Robert Logan of Restalrig entered into a secret bond, or pact, with John Napier, the enigmatic mathematician famed for his formulation of the means of calculation known as logarithms, and who in his day was darkly hinted to be a 'wizard.'

The pact between the pair was that Napier would search the castle for 'treasure' and '…do his utmost diligence to seek out, and by all craft and ingine to find out the same, and by the grace of God either find out the same, or make it sure that no such thing has been found there'.

If successful, Napier was to be rewarded with one third of any 'treasure' found – but no record of his success or otherwise has ever surfaced.

Had 'treasure' indeed been found, it did not save Sir Robert Logan of Restalrig from the fate that befell he and his family in the wake of another mysterious affair.

This was the Gowrie Conspiracy of August 5, 1600, the truth behind which has never been satisfactorily determined even up to the present day – although there is a consensus of opinion that it most likely had involved a plot to kidnap the king.

James VI had apparently been about to set off on his favourite pastime of hunting when he was approached by Alexander, the young Master of Ruthven, and brother of the Earl of Gowrie.

He had a strange tale to relate: he claimed he had discovered a man attempting to bury a cache of gold coins in a field outside Perth, and urged the king to come with him to meet the man and see the gold.

The avaricious James complied, and when he came to Gowrie House, in Perth, he was ushered into a turret room by the young Master.

The 'official' account of what subsequently transpired after the unsuspecting king entered the room is that the Master drew a dagger, telling his monarch he was going to kill him in revenge for his role in the death of his father.

James managed to shout for help from the window of the turret and John Ramsay, one of his trusted courtiers rushed in and stabbed the Master to death. The Earl of Gowrie, following close on the heels of the courtier and others who had dashed to the king's aid, was also stabbed to death.

Sir Robert Logan of Restalrig died in 1606, but two years after this George Sprot, who had been one of his servants, came forward with information that his master had been privy to a conspiracy along with the Earl of Gowrie and others to abduct the king.

Sprot was hanged for 'foreknowledge of the conspiracy', although serious doubts were cast on the veracity of his testimony.

As was not unusual in these dark times, Logan's corpse was exhumed and his bones actually put on trial in Edinburgh and, found guilty, the Logan estates forfeited.

In more peaceful times, John Logan was the journalist, author and Gaelic scholar born in Aberdeen in 1797, the son of a merchant.

It was thanks to generous patrons and through employment for a time with the Highland Society of London that he was able to make a living and study Gaelic culture.

Best known for his two-volume *The Scottish Gael, or Celtic Manners as preserved among the Highlanders*, first published in 1831 and based on walking tours he had undertaken throughout the Highlands and Islands, he died in London in 1872.

In the often cut-throat world of politics,

Graeme Andrew Logan is the leading British Conservative Party politician better known by his adopted name Michael Gove.

Born in 1967 in Aberdeen, it was not until a number of years later that he learned from his adoptive parents his biological mother had been a 23-year-old unmarried cookery demonstrator – in fact having believed he had been born in Edinburgh to an unmarried student.

Aged four months, he was adopted by Ernest Gove, who ran a fish processing business in Aberdeen, and his wife Christine, a laboratory assistant at Aberdeen University. The couple changed his name to Michael Andrew Gove and he went on to display academic skills that saw him being accepted for Oxford University, where he read English from 1985 to 1988.

It was here that he first met future Conservative Prime Minister Boris Johnson, helping him in his successful bid to be elected president of the Oxford Union – a post Gove also held after Johnson's tenure ended.

Embarking on a career in journalism as a trainee reporter with the *Aberdeen Press and Journal*, he later worked for other publications including *The Times* – as a leader writer, comment editor, news editor and assistant editor – *The Times Literary Supplement* and the *Spectator*.

Married to fellow journalist Sarah Vine, he entered politics in 2005 as MP (Member of Parliament) for the English constituency Surrey Heath, later holding government posts under Prime Minister David Cameron including Secretary of State for Education and Secretary of State for Justice.

Serving in other posts in the government of Prime Minister Theresa May, including Secretary of State for Environment, Food and Rural Affairs, he was also co-convener of the Vote Leave campaign in the 2016 referendum on EU membership, and has stood thrice for the leadership of his party.

This was most controversially in 2016 when, while campaign manager for Boris Johnson's bid for leadership, he suddenly withdrew his support and announced his own candidacy.

Failing in another leadership bid in 2019 in which Johnson was successful and subsequently became Prime Minister, following the general election later that year he was appointed by his erstwhile political rival as Chancellor of the Duchy of Lancaster – with responsibilities including chairing the UK/EU committee overseeing the Withdrawal Agreement.

Chapter four:

On the world stage

One of a family dynasty of entertainers, Georgina Allan was the Scots-American actress and singer better known by her stage name Ella Logan.

Born in Glasgow in 1910, she began performing as a child, later becoming a music hall band singer before making her London West End debut in 1930 in *Darling! I Love You*.

Immigrating to the United States and adopting the name by which she became famous, she signed a recording deal as a jazz singer and appeared in a number of Broadway productions throughout the 1930s and 1940s.

Entertaining troops in North Africa and Europe during the Second World War, she hit the Broadway stage again in 1947 in the original production of *Finian's Rainbow*, singing what became the famous *How Are Things in Glocca Morra?*

Establishing herself in the 1950s as an international night club performer, she died in 1969.

Her nephew was the Scottish entertainer, producer, director and theatre owner James Allan

Short, better known as **Jimmy Logan**, born in 1928 in the Dennistoun area of Glasgow.

With show business in his blood from an early age, his parents were John "Jack" Short and Mary Dalziel Short (née Allan), who performed as the music hall act Short and Dalziel, touring throughout Scotland, Northern Ireland and the United States.

Performing in sell-out seasons at the Metropole Theatre, Glasgow and The Theatre, Paisley, Logan became their house manager while, in 1944 he took to the stage in his own right in pantomime, later adopting his aunt's stage surname 'Logan'.

Maintaining his connection with pantomime throughout his life, he bought the Empress Theatre in Glasgow in 1964 and refurbished it as the New Metropole – which staged the first Scottish production of the rock musical *Hair!*

A major comedy star of television and film, his big screen credits include the 1972 *Carry On Abroad*, the 1999 *Captain Jack* and, along with fellow Glaswegian comic and actor Billy Connolly, the 1999 *The Debt Collector*.

A collector of memorabilia relating to the late Scottish entertainer Harry Lauder, now housed in Glasgow University's Scottish Theatre Archive, he died in 2001, while his own extensive archive of personal papers and other show business ephemera is held by the Royal Conservatoire of Scotland.

The recipient of an OBE for services to Scottish theatre and an honorary doctorate from Glasgow Caledonian University, he was the older brother of Annabelle Allan Short, better known as the Scots-American singer and actress **Annie Ross**.

Born in 1930, she was aged only four when she travelled to New York with her parents and shortly afterwards won a contract with MGM through a children's radio contest.

Staying in the United States when her parents returned home, she was taken under the wing of her aunt Ella Logan.

Aged only 14 when she wrote the song *Let's Fly* for a song-writing contest, it was subsequently recorded by Johnny Mercer and the Pied Pipers.

Changing her surname to 'Ross' – after her aunt told her she had an Irish grandmother of the name – in 1949 she went on to record the classic *Twisted*, based on a composition by saxophonist Wardell Gray, and toured and recorded with the trio Lambert, Hendricks and Ross.

After turning her talents to film, she had roles in the 1976 *Alfie Darling* and the 1983 *Superman III*, while also appearing in a number of stage productions.

Based on her relationship with her aunt and a tempestuous affair with the American comedian Lenny Bruce and her addiction for a time to heroin, *Twisted: The Annie Ross Story* was staged in 2006, while, eight years before her death in 2020, her life and times were the subject of the film documentary *No One But Me*.

Also on the stage, **Phyllis Logan** is the Scottish actress known for her roles from 1986 to 1993 in the television series *Lovejoy* and, from 2010 to 2015, in the popular television costume drama *Downton Abbey*.

Born in Paisley in 1956 and winner of the BAFTA Award for Most Promising Newcomer for the 1983 *Another Time, Another Place*, other big screen credits include the 1996 *Secrets and Lies* and, from 1997, *Shooting Fish*.

On American shores, **Jacqueline Logan** was the American actress of stage and screen who became a noted screenwriter.

Born in 1904 in Corsicana, Texas, her early screen credits from the silent era include the 1921 *The*

Perfect Crime, while she also had the role of Mary Magdalene in the 1927 Cecil B. De Mille classic *The King of Kings*.

Working for a time in Britain, she wrote the screenplay for the 1931 *Knock-Out* and, in the same year, wrote and directed *Strictly Business*; she died in 1983.

Born in 1987 in Auckland, New Zealand and of Maori descent, **Daniel Logan** is the actor known for his role Bobba Fett in the 2002 *Star Wars: Episode II – Attack of the Clones*.

Nominated for an Oscar Young Artist Award for Best Performance in a Feature Film (Supporting Actor) for his role, he was granted American citizenship in 2017.

Back on British shores, **Jenny Logan** is the English actress born in 1942.

Although having television acting credits that include *Pennies From Heaven* and *London's Burning*, she is best known as the housewife featured in a commercial for the carpet freshener Shake n' Vac.

Running on television from 1980 to 1986 and with the catchy jingle "do the Shake n' Vac, and put the freshness back", ITV has named it one of its best ever commercials.

Back on American shores, and behind the camera lens, **Joshua Logan III** was the award-winning stage and film director born in 1908 in Texarkana, Texas.

In addition to success with Broadway productions including the 1938 *On Borrowed Time* and, two years later, *Charley's Aunt*, he also co-wrote and directed *South Pacific*, which ran on stage from 1949 to 1954.

Sharing along with songwriters Richard Rodgers and Oscar Hammerstein the 1950 Pulitzer Prize for Drama for the production and an individual Tony Award for Best Director, on the big screen he directed the 1956 *Bus Stop*, starring Marilyn Monroe.

His autobiography *Movie Stars, Real People and Me* was published ten years before his death in 1988.

Bearers of the Logan name have also gained fame in the highly competitive world of sport.

In the rough and tumble of the rugby pitch, Kenneth McKerrow Logan is the Scotland former rugby union internationalist better known as **Kenny Logan**.

Born in Stirling in 1972 and beginning his rugby career with Stirling County, he played for

Glasgow Rugby after the professional era of the game began in 1986, later playing for other teams including Wasps – winners of the Anglo-Welsh Cup in 1999 and 2000 and the 2002-2003 Premiership Final.

The winner of 70 caps for his nation over a thirteen-year period and scoring 20 tries, he has spoken of his early struggles with dyslexia and how he found solace through sport – firstly through playing football and then rugby.

In 2001 he married the BBC sports presenter and former gymnast Gabrielle Nicol Logan (née Yorath), better known as **Gabby Logan**.

Born in 1973 in Leeds, the daughter of Welsh former football internationalist and manager Terry Yorath, she represented Wales at the 1990 Commonwealth Games and placed 11th in rhythmic gymnastics.

Retiring from gymnastics because of sciatica, she is now a familiar face on television screens presenting a range of sporting events.

Returning to the rugby pitch, **Scott Logan** is the Scotland former international rugby league player born in 1976 in New South Wales, Australia.

Having played as a prop for the Canberra Raiders and English teams including Hull and

Wigan Warriors, through his parentage he qualified to represent Scotland and was in the squad for the 2008 Rugby League World Cup.

In baseball, **Boone Logan**, born in 1984 in San Antonio, Texas, is the American former professional relief pitcher who played in Major League Baseball (MLB) for teams including the Chicago White Sox, Colorado Rockies and Milwaukee Brewers.

From sport to publishing, **Nick Logan** is the British journalist, editor and publisher who in 1980 founded the lifestyle magazine *The Face*.

Born in 1947 in Lincoln, he was also editor for a time of *New Musical Express* (*NME*) and creator of the other pop music title *Smash Hits*.

One rather unusual master of words is the Canadian research mathematician and champion Scrabble player **Adam Logan**, born in Kingston, Ontario, in 1975.

Winner of the 2005 World Scrabble Championship, he is also the only player to date to have won – between 1996 and 2016 – the Canadian Scrabble Championship five times.